BOOK 2 - Baritone B.C.

STANDARD OF EXCELLENCE

COMPREHENSIVE BAND METHOD

By Bruce Pearson

Dear Student:

Congratulations! You have successfully attained the first level in achieving a standard of excellence in music-making. By now, you have discovered that careful study and regular practice have brought you the joy and satisfaction of making beautiful music.

You are now ready to move to the next level in your music-making. I want to welcome you to STANDARD OF EXCELLENCE Book 2. I also want to wish you continued success and enjoyment.

Best wishes,

Bruce Pearson

Practicing - the key to EXCELLENCE!

▶ Make practicing part of your daily schedule. If you plan practicing as you do any other activity, you will find plenty of time for it.
▶ Try to practice in the same place every day. Choose a place where you can concentrate on making music. Start with a regular and familiar warm-up routine, including long tones and simple technical exercises. Like an athlete, you need to warm-up your mind and muscles before you begin performing.
▶ Set goals for every practice session. Keep track of your practice time and progress on the front cover Practice Journal.
▶ Practice the hard spots in your lesson assignment and band music over and over, until you can play them perfectly.
▶ Spend time practicing both alone and with the STANDARD OF EXCELLENCE recorded accompaniments.
▶ At the end of each practice session, play something fun.

ISBN 0-8497-5965-X

© 1993 Neil A. Kjos Music Company, 4380 Jutland Drive, San Diego, California.
International copyright secured. All rights reserved. Printed in the U. S. A.

KJOS NEIL A. KJOS MUSIC COMPANY, PUBLISHER   W22BC

REVIEW

B♭ MAJOR KEY SIGNATURE

1 WARM-UP - Band Arrangement

Andante

2 B♭ MAJOR SCALE SKILL

Moderato

Arpeggio   Chords

▶ Lines with a medal are *Achievement Lines.* The chart on page 47 can be used to record your progress.

3 BOTANY BAY   Page 40 ▶

Australian Folk Song

Moderato

▶ When you see a page number followed by an arrow, *Excellerate* to the page indicated for additional studies.

4 DRIVE TIME

Andante

5 SHEPHERD'S HEY

English Folk Song

Fine

Moderato

D.C. al Fine

REVIEW

E♭ MAJOR KEY SIGNATURE

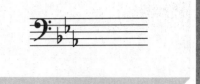

6 E♭ MAJOR SCALE SKILL

Moderato

Arpeggio   Chords

mf

▶ Are you playing with a good embouchure and hand position?

7 MOLLY MALONE

Irish Folk Song

Andante

1.   2.

mp   *f*   *mp*   *mp*   *rit.*

8 NO LOOKING BACK   Page 40 ▶

Moderato

mf

9 TURKISH MARCH

Wolfgang Amadeus Mozart (1756 - 1791)

Allegro

1.>   2.>

mf

10 HYMN OF THANKSGIVING - Band Arrangement

Johann Crüger (1598 - 1662)
arr. Bruce Pearson (b. 1942)

Andante

mf   *p*   *mf*

p

f   *mf*   *rit.*

4

REVIEW

F MAJOR KEY SIGNATURE

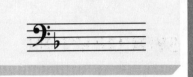

11 WARM-UP - Band Arrangement

Andante

12 F MAJOR SCALE SKILL

Moderato

Arpeggio   Chords

13 KNUCKLEBUSTER

Moderato

14 GIVE ME THAT OLD TIME RELIGION   Page 40 ➠   American Spiritual

Allegro

15 _____   Composer _____

your name

Moderato

▶ Compose an ending for this melody. Title and play your composition.

16 FOR BARITONES ONLY   Page 40 ➠

Allegro

| SYNCOPATION |  | A rhythmic effect which places emphasis on a weak or unaccented part of the measure. |
| INTERVAL |  | The distance between any two notes. |

17 **SYNCOPATION SENSATION**

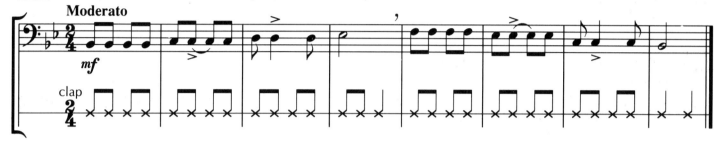

18 **THE RIDDLE SONG**

American Folk Song

▶ Write in the counting and clap the rhythm before you play.

19 **NOBODY KNOWS THE TROUBLE I'VE SEEN**

American Spiritual

20 **INTERVAL INQUIRY**

▶ Sing this exercise using the numbers before you play.

21 **GO FOR EXCELLENCE!**

American Folk Song

6

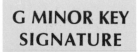

G MINOR KEY SIGNATURE

G minor has the same key signature as **B♭ major.**

TEMPO

Accelerando (accel.) - Gradually increase the tempo.

DIVISI

UNISON

Part of the section plays the top notes and part of the section plays the bottom notes.

Everyone plays the same notes.

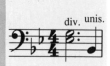

22 WARM-UP - Band Arrangement

Andante

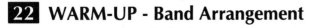

23 G NATURAL MINOR SCALE SKILL

Moderato

24 G HARMONIC MINOR SCALE SKILL — Page 40

Moderato

25 MINKA, MINKA

Ukrainian Folk Song

Moderato

2nd time - *accel.*

Hey!

26 LAREDO - Duet

Mexican Folk Song

Moderato

► Name the interval between the top and bottom notes of the last measure. _____

27 TURNING YOU LOOSE

Moderato

28 FOR BARITONES ONLY

Allegro

W22BC

DAL SEGNO AL FINE
(D.S. AL FINE)

Go back to the sign (𝄋) and play until the *Fine.*

JOYEUX NOËL
Band Arrangement

French Carol
arr. Chuck Elledge (b. 1961)

29 **GO FOR EXCELLENCE!**

W22BC

EIGHTH REST

𝄾 = ½ count in 2/4, 3/4, and 4/4 time.

An eighth rest is as long as an eighth note.

30 EIGHTH REST ON THE BEAT
Moderato

▶ Write in the counting and clap the rhythm before you play.

31 EIGHTH REST OFF THE BEAT
Moderato

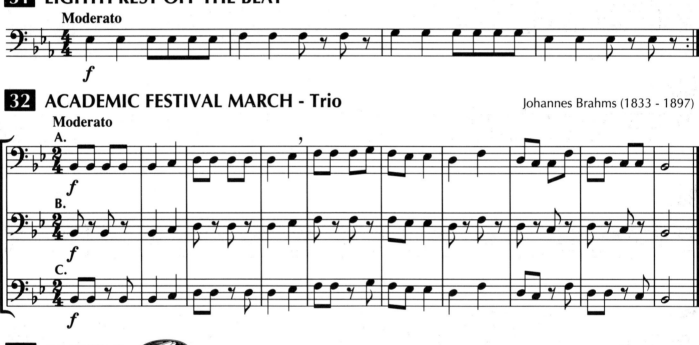

32 ACADEMIC FESTIVAL MARCH - Trio
Johannes Brahms (1833 - 1897)
Moderato

33 BREEZIN'
Allegro

34 YANKEE DOODLE - Duet
American Folk Song
Moderato

35 FOR BARITONES ONLY
Allegro

A♭ MAJOR KEY SIGNATURE

This key signature means play all B's as B flats, all E's as E flats, all A's as A flats, and all D's as D flats.

TEXTURES

Monophony - a single unaccompanied melody.

Polyphony - two or more melodies played at the same time.

36 A♭ MAJOR SCALE SKILL

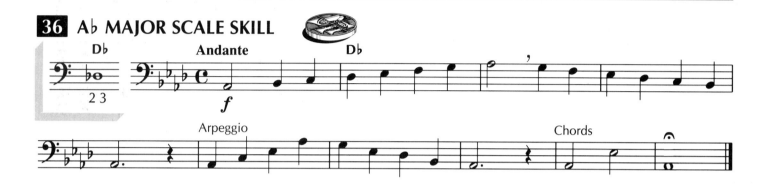

37 GREASED LIGHTNING

38 PARTNER SONGS - Duet

▶ For an example of monophony, play line A or line B alone. For an example of polyphony, play line A while someone else plays line B.

39 GO FOR EXCELLENCE!

Stephen Foster (1826 - 1864)

10

ENHARMONICS

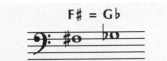

F♯ = G♭

Notes that sound the same but are written differently.

ARTICULATION

Staccato (dot placed above or below note) - Play short and detached.

TEMPO

Allegretto - light and lively; slightly slower than **Allegro.**

40 WARM-UP - Band Arrangement

41 CHROMATIC CAPERS

42 SHENANDOAH

Page 40

American Folk Song

43 THEME FROM SYMPHONY NO. 94

Franz Joseph Haydn (1732 - 1809)

44 PARADE OF THE TIN SOLDIERS

Léon Jessel (1871 - 1942)

45 FOR BARITONES ONLY

C MINOR KEY SIGNATURE

C minor has the same key signature as E♭ major.

ARTICULATIONS

Tenuto (line placed above or below note) - Sustain for full value.

legato

Legato - Play as smoothly as possible.

46 C NATURAL MINOR SCALE

Andante

mf

47 C HARMONIC MINOR SCALE

B

1 2

Andante

B

mf

48 MARCHE SLAV

Peter Ilyich Tchaikovsky (1840 - 1893)

Andante

mf legato

1. 2.

49 GREENSLEEVES

English Song

B

1 2 3

Moderato

B

mp legato

▶ Name the key in "Greensleeves." _____

50 JUBILATE

Wolfgang Amadeus Mozart (1756 - 1791)

Allegretto

mf

1. 2.

51 GO FOR EXCELLENCE!

Allegretto

mf

W22BC

12

| TEXTURE | **Melody and Accompaniment** - main melody is accompanied by chords or less important melodies called **countermelodies.** |

TIME SIGNATURE

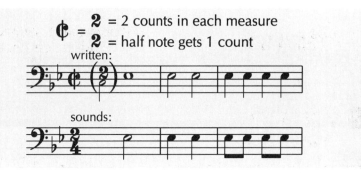

This time signature is called **cut time** or *alla breve*.

58 CUT AND PASTE

Moderato

mf

▶ Write in the counting and clap the rhythm before you play.

59 OATS, PEAS, BEANS

American Folk Song

Moderato

60 THE VICTORS

Fight Song

Allegro

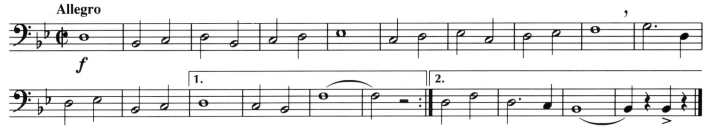

61 OVER EASY

Page 41 ▶

62 GO FOR EXCELLENCE!

John Philip Sousa (1854 - 1932)

Allegretto
"High School Cadets March"

ENHARMONICS

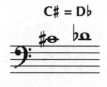

C# = Db

CHORD

fifth
third
root

Two or more pitches sounded
at the same time.

63 **WARM-UP - Band Arrangement**

64 **DANISH ROLL**

Danish Folk Song

65 **RUSSIAN SAILORS' DANCE**

Reinhold Glière (1875 - 1956)

66 **CHORD CAPERS**

▶ Listen for the different types of chords played by the full band.

67 **FOR BARITONES ONLY**

ENHARMONICS

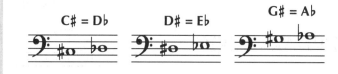

68 CHROMATIC SCALE SKILL

69 SAILING THE HIGH SEAS

70 CHROMATIC MARCH

Page 41 ⏵

71 MANHATTAN BEACH MARCH

John Philip Sousa (1854 - 1932)

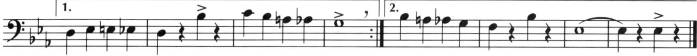

72 GO FOR EXCELLENCE!

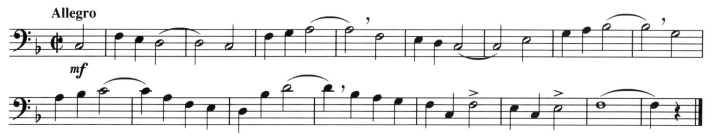

▶ Play using each of the following articulations: A. B. C. D.

DA CAPO AL CODA
(D.C. AL CODA)

Go back to the beginning and play until the coda sign (⊕). When you reach the coda sign, skip to the *Coda* (⊕).

ROCK ISLAND EXPRESS
Band Arrangement

Chuck Elledge (b. 1961)

TIME SIGNATURE

3 = 3 counts in each measure
8 = eighth note gets 1 count

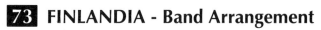

73 FINLANDIA - Band Arrangement

Jean Sibelius (1865 - 1957)
arr. Bruce Pearson (b. 1942)

Moderato

p legato

74 TRIPLE PLAY

Allegretto

▶ Write in the counting and clap the rhythm before you play.

75 WE THREE KINGS

Page 41 ▶

John H. Hopkins, Jr. (1820 - 1891)

Andante

▶ Name the key in "We Three Kings." _____

76 GO FOR EXCELLENCE!

Allegro

f legato

C MAJOR KEY SIGNATURE

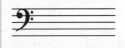

This key signature contains no sharps or flats.

TIME SIGNATURE

6
8

6 = 6 counts in each measure
8 = eighth note gets 1 count

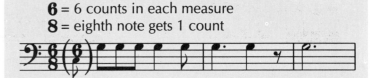

77 C MAJOR SCALE SKILL

Andante

Arpeggio   Chords

mf

78 OVER THE RIVER

Traditional

Allegro

f

1.

2.

▶ Draw in a breath mark at the end of each phrase.

79 OODLES OF NOODLES

Moderato

mf

80 UPS AND DOWNS

Allegretto

mp

▶ Write in the counting and draw in the bar lines before you play.

81 FOR BARITONES ONLY

Allegro

mf

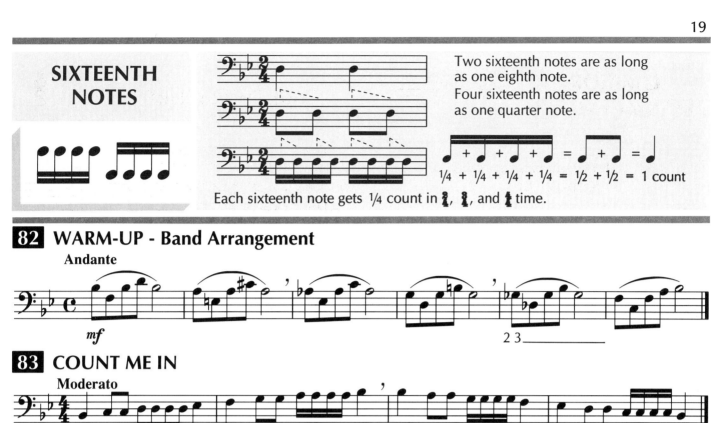

SIXTEENTH NOTES

Two sixteenth notes are as long as one eighth note.
Four sixteenth notes are as long as one quarter note.

$\frac{1}{4} + \frac{1}{4} + \frac{1}{4} + \frac{1}{4} = \frac{1}{2} + \frac{1}{2} = 1$ count

Each sixteenth note gets ¼ count in ♩, ♩, and ♩ time.

82 WARM-UP - Band Arrangement

Andante

mf

2 3

83 COUNT ME IN

Moderato

mf

▶ Write in the counting and clap the rhythm before you play.

84 KEMO KIMO

American Folk Song

Allegretto

p *f* *p* *f*

p *f*

85 FRENCH MARCHING SONG

French Folk Song

Allegro

f

1. 2.

▶ Name the interval between the first and second notes. _____

86 FENG YANG SONG   Page 41 ▶

Chinese Folk Song

Moderato

mp

87 GO FOR EXCELLENCE!

Patrick Gilmore (1829 - 1892)

Allegro

"When Johnny Comes Marching Home"

mp *mf*

f

mp

88 LOOBY LOO — Anonymous

▶ Name the key in "Looby Loo."_____

89 THE THUNDERER — John Philip Sousa (1854 - 1932)

90 LISTEN TO THE MOCKINGBIRD — Alice Hawthorne (1827 - 1902)

91 GIVE MY REGARDS TO BROADWAY — George M. Cohan (1878 - 1942)

92 FOR BARITONES ONLY — Page 41

EIGHTH/SIXTEENTH NOTE COMBINATIONS

93 CHESTER - Band Arrangement

William Billings (1746 - 1800)
arr. Bruce Pearson (b. 1942)

94 STEADY AS YOU GO - Duet

95 TIRRA LIRRA LOO

Canadian Folk Song

▶ Write in the counting and clap the rhythm before you play.

96 GO FOR EXCELLENCE!

American Folk Song

"Big Rock Candy Mountain"

TURKISH MARCH
from "The Ruins of Athens"
Solo with Piano Accompaniment

Ludwig van Beethoven (1770 - 1827)
arr. Bruce Pearson (b. 1942)

97 BLAZIN'

▶ Name the interval between the first and second notes. ——————————

98 AMERICAN PATROL

Frank W. Meacham (1856 - 1909)

99 KERRY DANCE

Page 41 ▶

Irish Folk Song

100 GAVOTTE

James Hook (1746 - 1827)

101 FOR BARITONES ONLY

SINGLE SIXTEENTH NOTE

A single sixteenth note is half as long as an eighth note.

$\flat$ = ¼ count in ⁴⁄₄, ³⁄₄, and ²⁄₄ time.

DOTTED EIGHTH NOTE

A dot after a note adds half the value of the note.

DOTTED EIGHTH/ SIXTEENTH NOTE COMBINATION

102 **DOTS OF FUN**

Moderato

103 **LITTLE BROWN JUG - Duet**

Joseph Eastburn Winner (1837 - 1918)

Allegro

▶ Write in the counting and clap the rhythm before you play.

104 **OUR BOYS WILL SHINE TONIGHT**

College Song

Allegretto

▶ Draw in a breath mark at the end of each phrase.

105 _____ Composer _____ your name

▶ Compose an ending for this melody. Be sure to use the rhythm. Title and play your composition.

106 **GO FOR EXCELLENCE!**

Georges Bizet (1838 - 1875)

Allegro

"Farandole from L'Arlesienne Suite"

107 CUCKOO SONG Page 41 ▶   Austrian Folk Song

108 MARCH MILITAIRE   Franz Schubert (1797 - 1828)

to Coda

D.C. al Coda   *Coda*

109 ST. ANTHONY CHORALE   Franz Joseph Haydn (1732 - 1809)

D.C. al Fine

110 _____   Composer _____

your name

a.   b.   c.   d.

▶ Arrange these melodic pieces in any order to build a tune you like. You may use pieces more than once. Title and play your composition.

111 FOR BARITONES ONLY

A **Andante**   B   C

▶ Play each of the lip slur patterns using the following fingerings: **0; 2; 1; 1 2; 2 3; 1 3; 1 2 3.**
You will be moving down a half step with each fingering.

EIGHTH NOTE TRIPLET

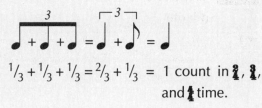

TEMPO

Maestoso - majestically

112 TRIPLE TREAT

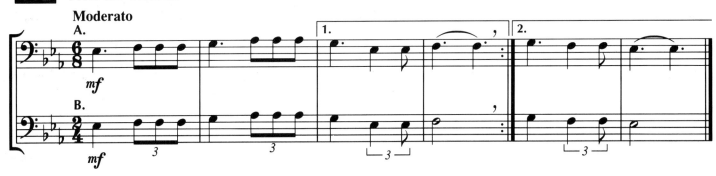

113 STARS OF THE HEAVENS - Duet   Page 41 ▶   Mexican Folk Song

114 LIGHT CAVALRY OVERTURE   Franz von Suppé (1819 - 1895)

115 GO FOR EXCELLENCE!   Charles Gounod (1818 - 1893)

"Soldiers' Chorus from Faust"

116 HERE WE COME A-WASSAILING

English Folk Song

117 THEME FROM "ZAMPA"

Ferdinand Herold (1791 - 1833)

118 GO FOR EXCELLENCE!

Peter Ilyich Tchaikovsky (1840 - 1893)

"March from the Nutcracker"

CABO RICO

Band Arrangement

Chuck Elledge (b. 1961)

W22BC

RUDIMENTAL REGIMENT
Band Arrangement

Bruce Pearson (b. 1942)
and Chuck Elledge (b. 1961)

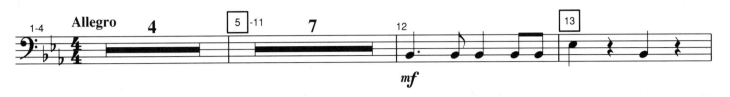

31

W22BC

SUMMER'S RAIN

Band Arrangement

Chuck Elledge (b. 1961)

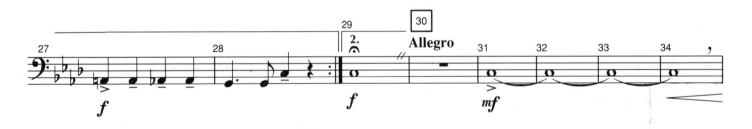

FRENCH MARKET BUZZARDS MARCH

Band Arrangement

Liberato Gallo
arr. Wendy Barden (b. 1955)

W22BC

ROMANZA

Ensemble

Ludwig van Beethoven, Op. 40 (1770 - 1827)
arr. Janice Strobl Kersey (b. 1959)

Baritone

HORNPIPE from "Water Music"

Ensemble

Baritone

George Frideric Handel (1685 - 1759)
arr. Janice Strobl Kersey (b. 1959)

mf - 1st time
f - 2nd time

rit. _ _ _ _ _ _ _ _ _ _ _ _ _

MINUET AND BOURRÉE

Solo with Piano Accompaniment

Minuet

George Frideric Handel (1685 - 1759)
arr. Bruce Pearson (b. 1942)

Bourrée

EXCELLERATORS - FOR BARITONES ONLY

EXCELLERATORS - FOR BARITONES ONLY

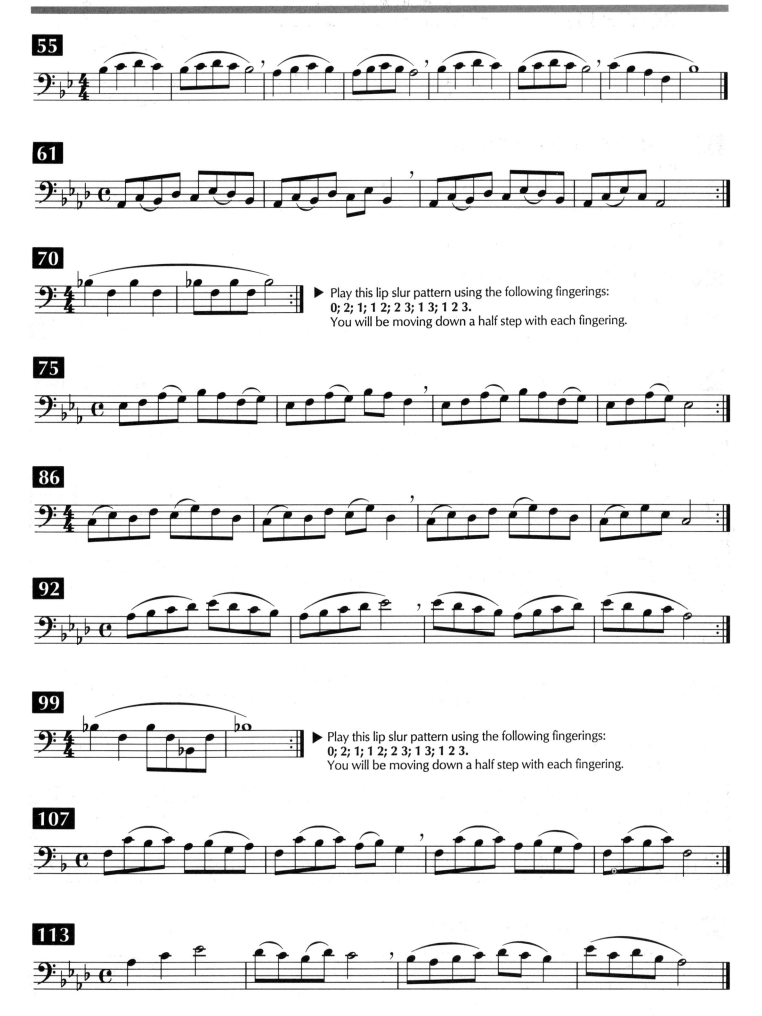

70 ▶ Play this lip slur pattern using the following fingerings:
0; 2; 1; 1 2; 2 3; 1 3; 1 2 3.
You will be moving down a half step with each fingering.

99 ▶ Play this lip slur pattern using the following fingerings:
0; 2; 1; 1 2; 2 3; 1 3; 1 2 3.
You will be moving down a half step with each fingering.

SCALE STUDIES

Bb MAJOR SCALE

G HARMONIC MINOR SCALE

Eb MAJOR SCALE

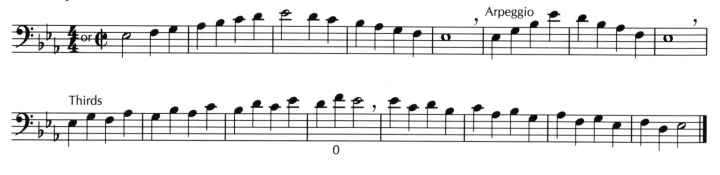

C HARMONIC MINOR SCALE

SCALE STUDIES

F MAJOR SCALE

Aᵇ MAJOR SCALE

C MAJOR SCALE

CHROMATIC SCALE

RHYTHM STUDIES

RHYTHM STUDIES

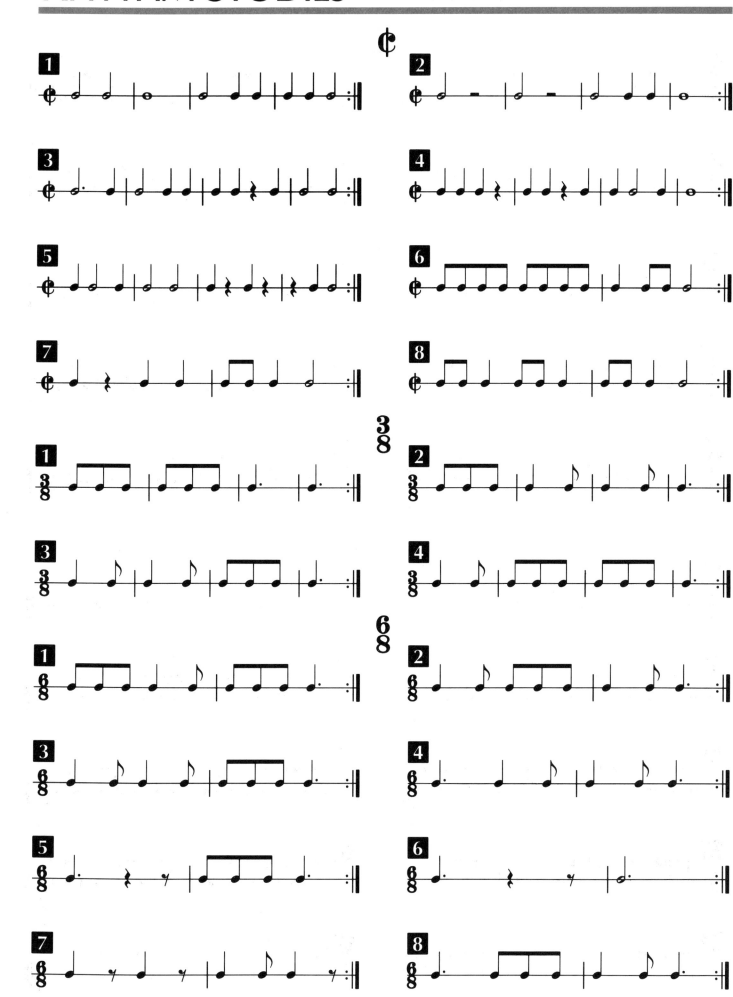

GLOSSARY/INDEX

Accelerando (accel.) (p.6) . . . . gradually increase the tempo

Alla Breve (p.13) . . . . same as cut time

Allegretto (p.10) . . . . light and lively; slightly slower than **Allegro**

Barden, Wendy (pp.22-23, 36-37) . . . . . American music educator and arranger (b. 1955)

Beethoven, Ludwig van (p. 36) . . . . . . German composer (1770-1827)

Billings, William (p.21) . . . . American composer (1746-1800)

Bizet, Georges (pp.12, 25) . . . . French composer (1838-1875)

Brahms, Johannes (p.8) . . . . German composer (1833-1897)

Chord (pp.2-4, 9, 14, 18) . . . . two or more pitches sounded at the same time

Chromatic Scale (pp.15, 43) . . . . scale of half steps

Cohan, George M. (p.20) . . . . American composer (1878-1942)

Countermelody (p.12) . . . . a less important melody that can be played along with the main melody

Crüger, Johann (p.3) . . . . German composer (1598-1662)

Cut Time (alla breve) (p.13) ¢ or $\frac{2}{2}$ . . a time signature indicating two counts in each measure, the half note gets one count

Da Capo al Coda (p.16) *D. C. al Coda* . go back to the beginning and play until the coda sign (⊕). When you reach the coda sign, skip to the *Coda* (⊕)

Dal Segno al Fine (p.7) *D. S. al Fine* . . go back to the 𝄋 sign and play until the *Fine*

Divisi (p.6) . . . . part of the section plays the top notes and part of the section plays the bottom notes

Elledge, Chuck (pp.7, 16, 29-33) . . . . . American composer/arranger (b. 1961)

Enharmonics (pp.10, 14-15) . . . . notes that sound the same but are written differently

Foster, Stephen (p.9) . . . . American composer (1826-1864)

Gallo, Liberato (pp.34-35) . . . . Italian composer

Gilmore, Patrick (p.19) . . . . American composer (1829-1892)

Glière, Reinhold (p.14) . . . . Russian composer (1875-1956)

Gounod, Charles (p.27) . . . . French composer (1818-1893)

Handel, George Frideric (pp. 37-39) . . . German composer (1685-1759)

Hawthorne, Alice (p.20) . . . . American composer (1827-1902)

Haydn, Franz Joseph (pp.10, 26) . . . . . Austrian composer (1732-1809)

Herold, Ferdinand (p.28) . . . . French composer (1791-1833)

Hook, James (p.24) . . . . English composer (1746-1827)

Hopkins, John H., Jr. (p.17) . . . . American composer (1820-1891)

Interval (p.5) . . . . distance between two notes

Jessel, Léon (p.10) . . . . German composer (1871-1942)

Kersey, Janice Strobl (pp.36-37) . . . . . . American music editor and arranger (b. 1959)

Legato (p.11) . . . . play as smoothly as possible

Maestoso (p.27) . . . . majestically

Meacham, Frank W. (p.24) . . . . American composer (1856-1909)

Melody (p.12) . . . . an organized succession of tones

Monophony (p.9) . . . . a single unaccompanied melody

Mozart, Wolfgang Amadeus (pp.3,11) . . . . Austrian composer (1756-1791)

Pearson, Bruce . . . . American music educator/composer/ arranger (b. 1942)

Polyphony (p.9) . . . . two or more melodies played at the same time

Schubert, Franz (p.26) . . . . Austrian composer (1797-1828)

Sibelius, Jean (p.17) . . . . Finnish composer (1865-1957)

Sousa, John Philip (pp.13, 15, 20) . . . . American composer (1854-1932)

Staccato (p.10) ♩ . . . . a dot placed above or below note meaning to play short and detached

Suppé, Franz von (p.27) . . . . Belgian composer (1819-1895)

Syncopation (p.5) ♪♩♪ . . . . a rhythmic effect which places emphasis on a weak or unaccented part of the measure

Tchaikovsky, Peter Ilyich (pp.11, 28) . . Russian composer (1840-1893)

Tenuto (p.11) ♩ . . . . a line placed above or below note meaning to sustain for full value

Texture (p.12) . . . . the character of a composition as determined by the relationship of its melodies, countermelodies, and/or chords

Unison (p.6) . . . . everyone plays the same notes

Winner, Joseph Eastburn (p.25) . . . . . . American composer (1837-1918)

STANDARD OF

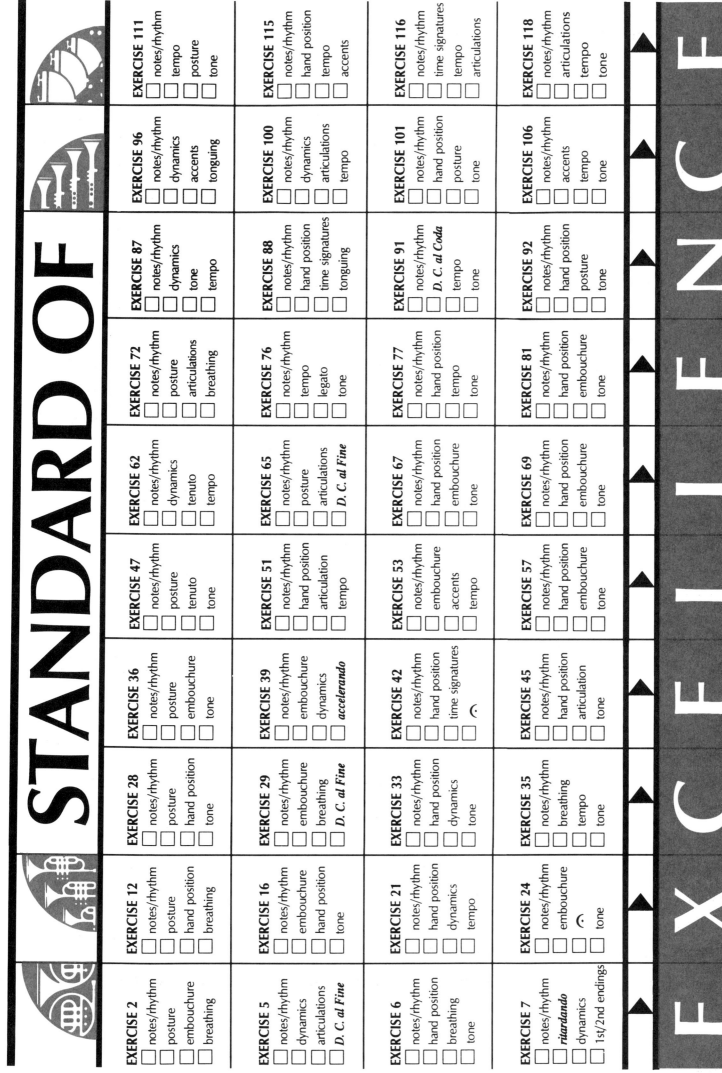

EXERCISE 2
- [ ] notes/rhythm
- [ ] posture
- [ ] embouchure
- [ ] breathing

EXERCISE 5
- [ ] notes/rhythm
- [ ] dynamics
- [ ] articulations
- [ ] *D. C. al Fine*

EXERCISE 6
- [ ] notes/rhythm
- [ ] hand position
- [ ] breathing
- [ ] tone

EXERCISE 7
- [ ] notes/rhythm
- [ ] *ritardando*
- [ ] dynamics
- [ ] 1st/2nd endings

EXERCISE 12
- [ ] notes/rhythm
- [ ] posture
- [ ] hand position
- [ ] breathing

EXERCISE 16
- [ ] notes/rhythm
- [ ] embouchure
- [ ] hand position
- [ ] tone

EXERCISE 21
- [ ] notes/rhythm
- [ ] hand position
- [ ] dynamics
- [ ] tempo

EXERCISE 24
- [ ] notes/rhythm
- [ ] embouchure
- [ ] ⌢
- [ ] tone

EXERCISE 28
- [ ] notes/rhythm
- [ ] posture
- [ ] hand position
- [ ] tone

EXERCISE 29
- [ ] notes/rhythm
- [ ] embouchure
- [ ] breathing
- [ ] *D. C. al Fine*

EXERCISE 33
- [ ] notes/rhythm
- [ ] hand position
- [ ] dynamics
- [ ] tone

EXERCISE 35
- [ ] notes/rhythm
- [ ] breathing
- [ ] tempo
- [ ] tone

EXERCISE 36
- [ ] notes/rhythm
- [ ] posture
- [ ] embouchure
- [ ] tone

EXERCISE 39
- [ ] notes/rhythm
- [ ] embouchure
- [ ] dynamics
- [ ] *accelerando*

EXERCISE 42
- [ ] notes/rhythm
- [ ] hand position
- [ ] time signatures
- [ ] ⌢

EXERCISE 45
- [ ] notes/rhythm
- [ ] hand position
- [ ] articulation
- [ ] tone

EXERCISE 47
- [ ] notes/rhythm
- [ ] posture
- [ ] tenuto
- [ ] tone

EXERCISE 51
- [ ] notes/rhythm
- [ ] hand position
- [ ] articulation
- [ ] tempo

EXERCISE 53
- [ ] notes/rhythm
- [ ] embouchure
- [ ] accents
- [ ] tempo

EXERCISE 57
- [ ] notes/rhythm
- [ ] hand position
- [ ] embouchure
- [ ] tone

EXERCISE 62
- [ ] notes/rhythm
- [ ] dynamics
- [ ] tenuto
- [ ] tempo

EXERCISE 65
- [ ] notes/rhythm
- [ ] posture
- [ ] articulations
- [ ] *D. C. al Fine*

EXERCISE 67
- [ ] notes/rhythm
- [ ] hand position
- [ ] embouchure
- [ ] tone

EXERCISE 69
- [ ] notes/rhythm
- [ ] hand position
- [ ] embouchure
- [ ] tone

EXERCISE 72
- [ ] notes/rhythm
- [ ] posture
- [ ] articulations
- [ ] breathing

EXERCISE 76
- [ ] notes/rhythm
- [ ] tempo
- [ ] legato
- [ ] tone

EXERCISE 77
- [ ] notes/rhythm
- [ ] hand position
- [ ] tempo
- [ ] tone

EXERCISE 81
- [ ] notes/rhythm
- [ ] hand position
- [ ] embouchure
- [ ] tone

EXERCISE 87
- [ ] notes/rhythm
- [ ] dynamics
- [ ] tone
- [ ] tempo

EXERCISE 88
- [ ] notes/rhythm
- [ ] hand position
- [ ] time signatures
- [ ] tonguing

EXERCISE 91
- [ ] notes/rhythm
- [ ] *D. C. al Coda*
- [ ] tempo
- [ ] tone

EXERCISE 92
- [ ] notes/rhythm
- [ ] hand position
- [ ] posture
- [ ] tone

EXERCISE 96
- [ ] notes/rhythm
- [ ] dynamics
- [ ] accents
- [ ] tonguing

EXERCISE 100
- [ ] notes/rhythm
- [ ] dynamics
- [ ] articulations
- [ ] tempo

EXERCISE 101
- [ ] notes/rhythm
- [ ] hand position
- [ ] posture
- [ ] tone

EXERCISE 106
- [ ] notes/rhythm
- [ ] accents
- [ ] tempo
- [ ] tone

EXERCISE 111
- [ ] notes/rhythm
- [ ] tempo
- [ ] posture
- [ ] tone

EXERCISE 115
- [ ] notes/rhythm
- [ ] hand position
- [ ] tempo
- [ ] accents

EXERCISE 116
- [ ] notes/rhythm
- [ ] time signatures
- [ ] tempo
- [ ] articulations

EXERCISE 118
- [ ] notes/rhythm
- [ ] articulations
- [ ] tempo
- [ ] tone

EXCELLENCE

THE BARITONE & EUPHONIUM

Baritone

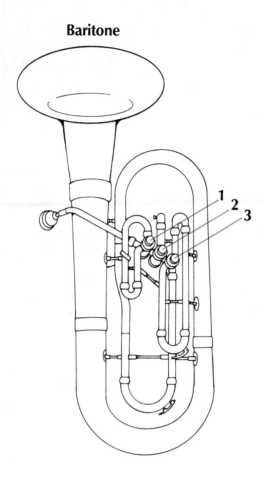

Euphonium

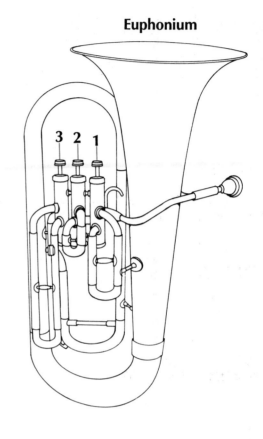

BARITONE CHECKLIST

- ☐ Sitting up straight
- ☐ Head erect
- ☐ Left hand and wrist position correct
- ☐ Right hand and wrist position correct
- ☐ Baritone correctly positioned in relation to body
- ☐ Fingers gently curved

- ☐ Elbows away from body
- ☐ Proper mouthpiece placement
- ☐ Corner of lips firm and center relaxed
- ☐ Chin flat and pointed
- ☐ Breathing properly
- ☐ Relaxed buzz

BARITONE SURVIVAL KIT

- ☐ soft, clean cloth
- ☐ valve oil
- ☐ pencil
- ☐ band music

- ☐ mouthpiece cleaning brush
- ☐ slide grease
- ☐ method book
- ☐ music stand